Vocal Selections

Grease

A Publication of
EDWIN H. MORRIS & COMPANY
A Division of
MPL COMMUNICATIONS, INC.

Exclusively Distributed By
HAL•LEONARD CORPORATION
7777 W. Bluemound Rd. P.O. Box 13819 Milwaukee, WI 53213

ISBN 0-88188-082-5

Barry & Fran Weissler
Jujamcyn Theaters

present

The **Tommy Tune** Production of
GREASE

Book, Music and Lyrics by
Jim Jacobs and Warren Casey

with
Ricky Paull Goldin Susan Wood
Sam Harris Marcia Lewis Billy Porter

Michelle Blakely Brian Bradley Paul Castree Hunter Foster Carlos Lopez
Megan Mullally Jason Opsahl Sandra Purpuro Heather Stokes Jessica Stone

Clay Adkins Melissa Bell Patrick Boyd Patti D'Beck Katy Grenfell Ned Hannah Denis Jone
Janice Lorraine Holt Brian Paul Mendoza Allison Metcalf H. Hylan Scott II Lorna Shane

and

Rosie O'Donnell

Scenic Design	Costume Design	Lighting Design
John Arnone	Willa Kim	Howell Binkley

Hair Design	Sound Design	Associate Choreographer	Casting
Patrik D. Moreton	Tom Morse	Jerry Mitchell	Stuart Howard & Amy Schecter, C.S.

Musical Direction, Vocal and Dance Music Arrangements	Orchestrations	Musical Coordinator
John McDaniel	Steve Margoshes	John Monaco

Production Stage Manager	Technical Supervisor	Press Representative	New York Press Representative
Craig Jacobs	Arthur Siccardi	Anita Dloniak	The Pete Sanders Group

Produced in Association with	Associate Producer	General Manager
PACE Theatrical Group	Alecia Parker	Charlotte W. Wilcox

Directed and Choreographed by
Jeff Calhoun

Grease

Jessica Stone (Frenchy), Sam Harris (Doody), Ricky Paull Goldin (Danny), Megan Mullally (Marty) and Hunter Foster (Roger)

Photo: Stan Schnier and Carmen Schiavone

Sam Harris (Doody) and Jessica Stone (Frenchy)

Photo: Carmen Schiavone

Marcia Lewis (Miss Lynch) and Michelle Blakely (Patty Simcox)

Photo: Carmen Schiavone

MEGAN MULLALLY (MARTY)

Photo: Stan Schnier and Carmen Schiavone

Ricky Paull Golden (Danny) and Susan Wood (Sandy)

Photo: Stan Schnier and Carmen Schiavone

JASON OPSAHL (KENICKIE)

Photo: Stan Schnier and Carmen Schiavone

Jason Opsahl (Kenickie) and Rosie O' Donneel (Rizzo)

Photo: Stan Schnier and Carmen Schiavone

Alma Mater

Lyric and Music by WARREN CASEY
and JIM JACOBS

C F D
rest from world - ly mat - ters, in pal-ace or in hov-el I may
G G7 C A♭
dwell, And tho' my bed be silk or tat - ters, my dreams shall
B♭ B♭7 E♭ C
al-ways be of thee, Ry - dell. Thru all the years, Ry - dell, and
F D G D
tears, Ry - dell, we give three cheers, Ry - dell, for

G
G7
C
A♭
thee. Thru ev-'ry-thing, Ry-dell, we cling, Ry-dell, and
B♭
B♭7
E♭
sing, Ry-dell to thee.

I saw a dead skunk on the highway
And I was goin' crazy from the smell
'Cause when the wind was blowin' my way
It smelt just like the halls of old Rydell.

And if you gotta use the toilet,
And later you start to scratch like hell,
Take off your underwear and boil it,
'Cause you got memories of old Rydell.

I can't explain, Rydell
This pain, Rydell
Is it ptomaine, Rydell gave me?
Is it V.D., Rydell
Could it be, Rydell,
You ought to see the faculty.

If Mister Clean, Rydell, has seen Rydell,
He'd just turn green and disappear.
I'm out-ta luck, Rydell, dead duck, Rydell
I'm stuck, Rydell, right here.

Summer Nights

Lyric and Music by WARREN CASEY
and JIM JACOBS

1.2.
A B Em A
drift - ing, a - way, too uh oh, those Sum - mer Nights.
some-things be - gun then uh oh, those Sum - mer Nights.
don't mean a thing but
D G
Chorus: Well - a, well - a, well - a uh, Boys: Tell me more, tell me
Well - a, well - a, well - a uh, Girls: Tell me more, tell me
E A D G
more, did you get ver - y far? Girls: Tell me more, tell me
more, was it love at first sight? Boys: Tell me more, tell me
E A D G A G
more like, does he have a car?
more did she put up a fight?

3
Em A B♭ E♭ A♭
uh oh, the Sum-mer Nights.
Boys: Tell me more, tell me
F B♭ E♭ A♭
more, like, you don't have to brag.
Girls: Tell me more, tell me
F B♭ E♭ A♭
more, 'cause he sounds like a drag.
Chorus: (Shu-da bop-bop, shu-da bop-bop,
B♭ A♭ E♭ A♭
shu-da bop-bop, shu-da bop-bop.)
Girl: He got friend-ly

Bb Ab Eb Ab Bb Ab
hold-ing my hand, Boy: She got friend-ly down on the sand.
Eb Ab Bb C F Bb
Girl: He was sweet just turn-ed eigh-teen. Boy: She was good, you
F Bb Bb7 Eb Ab Bb C
know what I mean. Both: Sum-mer heat, boy and girl meet, then,
Fm Bb B
uh oh, those Sum-mer Nights.

E A F♯ B
Girls: Tell me more, tell me more, how much dough did he spend?
E A F♯ B
Boys: Tell me more, tell me more, could she get me a friend?
E A E♭ A♭ B♭ A♭
Girl: It turned cold-er that's where it ends.
E♭ A♭ B♭ A♭ E♭ A♭
Boy: So I told her we'd still be friends.
Girl: Then we made
3
3

Bb C E A E A
our true love vow - ow. Boy: Won-der what she's do-in' now - ow.
Lightly
D G A B
Both: Sum-mer dreams ripped at the seams. But
Em A Db D G D
oh, those Sum-mer Nights.
Chorus: Tell me more, Tell me more.

Those Magic Changes

Lyric and Music by WARREN CASEY
and JIM JACOBS

Light "Rock" feel

Am
F
sends a thrill right through me, 'Cause those chords re-mind me of the
G7
C
Am
night that I first fell in love to Those Mag-ic Chan-ges,
F
G7
C
my heart ar-ran-ges a mel-o-dy that's
Am
F
G7
nev-er the same, a mel-o-dy, that's call-ing your name and begs you,

C Am F
please, come back to me. Please, re-
G7 C Am
turn to me, Don't go a-way a-gain, oh, make them play a-gain the mu-sic
F G7 C
I wan-na hear as once a-gain, you whis-per in my ear.
Am F G7
Oh, my dar-har-lin'.

C
Am
F
G7
C C C_ C C C A A A_ A min-or F F F_ F F F G G G_ G sev-en.
C
Am
F
I'll be wait-ing by the ra-di-o,_ you'll come back_ to me some
G7
C
Am
day, I know; Been so lone-some since your last good-bye,_
F
G7
CHORUS
C
But, I'm sing-ing as I cry-ay-ay-ay. While the bass is sound-ing,

Am
F
while the drums are pound - ing, Beat - ing of my bro - ken heart will
G7
C
climb to first place on the chart, Oooh, my heart ar -
3
Am
F
G7
ran-ges, oooh, Those Mag-ic Chan-ges,
3
C
Am
F
Oooh, o - o - o - oh oh,
Chorus:
(C C C C C C
A A A A min - or
F F F F F F

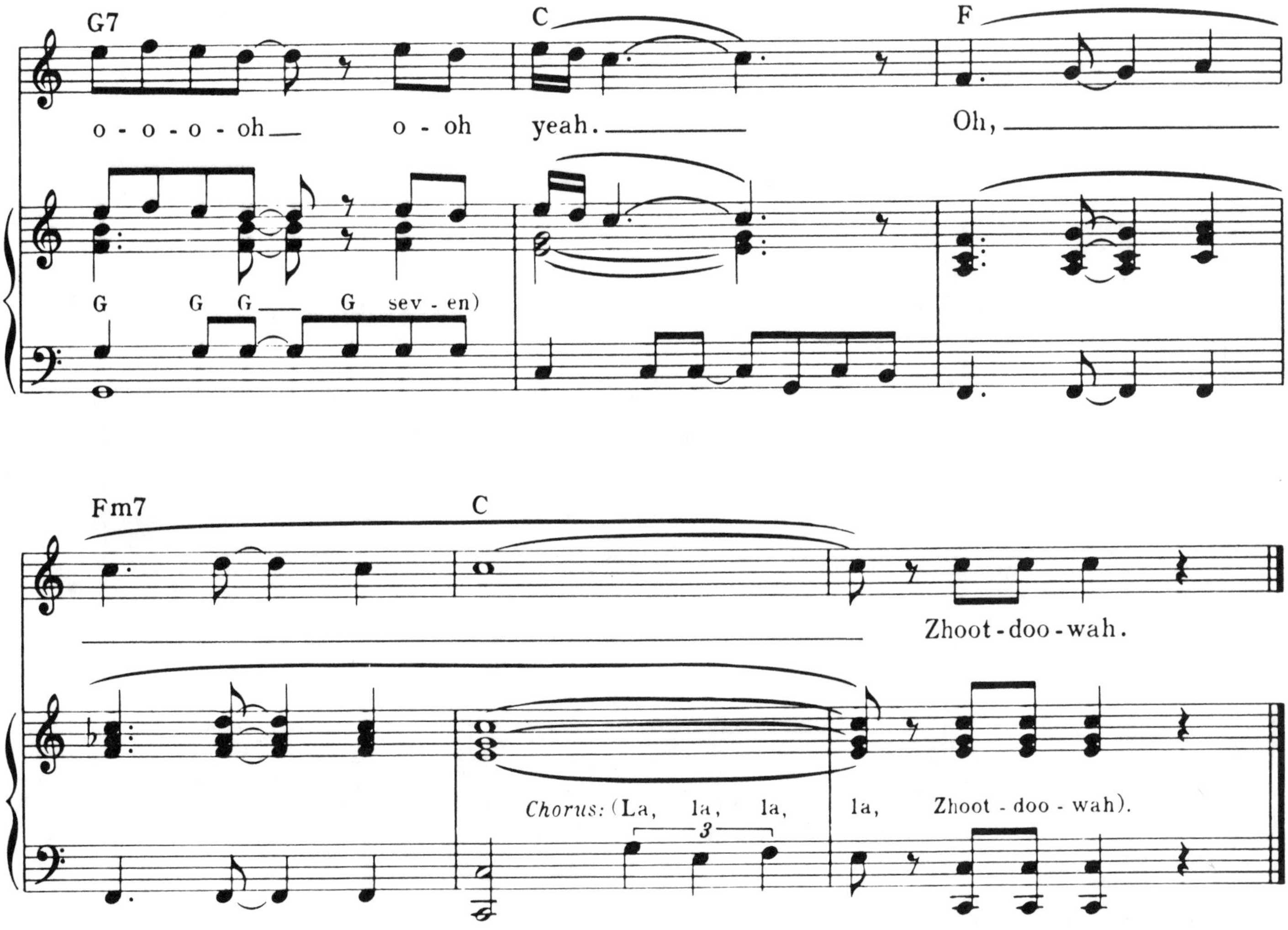
G7
C
F
o-o-o-oh o-oh yeah.
Oh,
G G G G sev-en)
Fm7
C
Zhoot-doo-wah.
Chorus: (La, la, la, la, Zhoot-doo-wah).
3

Freddy, My Love

Lyric and Music by WARREN CASEY
and JIM JACOBS

Slow Rock tempo
mf
D
Dmaj7
G
A7
1. Fred - dy, My Love, I miss you more than words can say,
2. (Fred - dy, you) know, your ab - sence makes me feel so blue;
3. (Fred - dy, you'll) see, you'll hold me in your arms some day;
mp
D
Dmaj7
B7sus4
B7
Fred - dy, My Love, please keep in touch while you're a - way.
That's o - kay, though, your pre - sents make me think of you.
And I will be wear - ing your lace - y loun - je - ray,

Em7 Em7-5 A7 A
Hear-ing from you can make the day ___ so much bet-ter,
My ma will have a heart at - tack ___ when she catch-es
Think-ing a - bout it my heart's pound - ing al - read - y,
F♯m D7 B7sus 4 B7
Get-ting a sou - ven - ir or may - be a let - ter
those ped-al push - ers with the black ___ leath-er patch-es,
Know-ing when you come home, we're bound ___ to go stead - y,
Em7 Gm/Cbass D/Abass G A7
I real - ly flipped o - ver the gray ___ cash-mere sweat-er, Fred-dy, My
Oh, how I wish I had a jack - et that match-es, Fred-dy, My
And throw your ser - vice _ pay a - round ___ like con - fet - ti, Fred-dy, My
D to Coda Dmaj7 G 1 A7 D
Love, Fred-dy, My Love, Fred-dy, My Love, Fred-dy My Lo-ove. Fred-dy, you
Love, Fred-dy, My Love, Fred-dy, My Love, Fred-dy My
Love, Fred-dy, My

2
D D7 G A7
Lo - ove. Don't keep your letters from me I
F♯m D7 B♭6 Am
thrill to ev-'ry line; Your spell-ing's kind-a crum-my, but,
Dm Dm7 Dm6 Em7-5 A7
hon-ey, so is mine. I trea-sure ev-'ry gift-ie, the
Dm G7 C Bm7
ring is real-ly nift-y, you say it cost you fif-ty, so you're

Em7
A7
D
D.S. al Coda
thrift - y, I don't mind, Oohh, oh! Fred - dy you'll
CODA
Dmaj7
G
A7
D
Repeat and fade out
Love, Fred - dy, My Love, Fred - dy, My Lo - ove. Fred - dy, My

Greased Lightnin'

Lyric and Music by WARREN CASEY
and JIM JACOBS

G
F
C
know with-out a doubt I'll be real - ly mak - in' out in Greased Light-nin'.
know that I ain't brag-gin', she's a real ___ drag-on wag-on, My Greased Light-nin'.
Go, go, go,
G
C
go, go, go, go, go, go, go, go,
Go Greased Light-nin', you're burn-in' up the quar-ter mile,
F
Greased Light-nin', go ___ Greased Light - nin'.
Yeah, Greased Light-nin', you're
C
coast-in' through the heat lap trial ___
You are su -
Greased Light-nin', go ___ Greased Light-nin'.

G
F
1 C
preme, the chicks-'ll cream for Greased Light-nin'.
Uh, huh!
Uh huh!
Go, go, go,
G
2 C
D.𝄋 3rd ending
I'll have me Light-nin'.
go, go, go, go, go, go, go, go,
Go, go, go,
go, go, go, go. go, go, go, go.
3 C
Light - nin'.
Yeah!
Light - nin' Light - nin', Light - nin' Light - nin'.

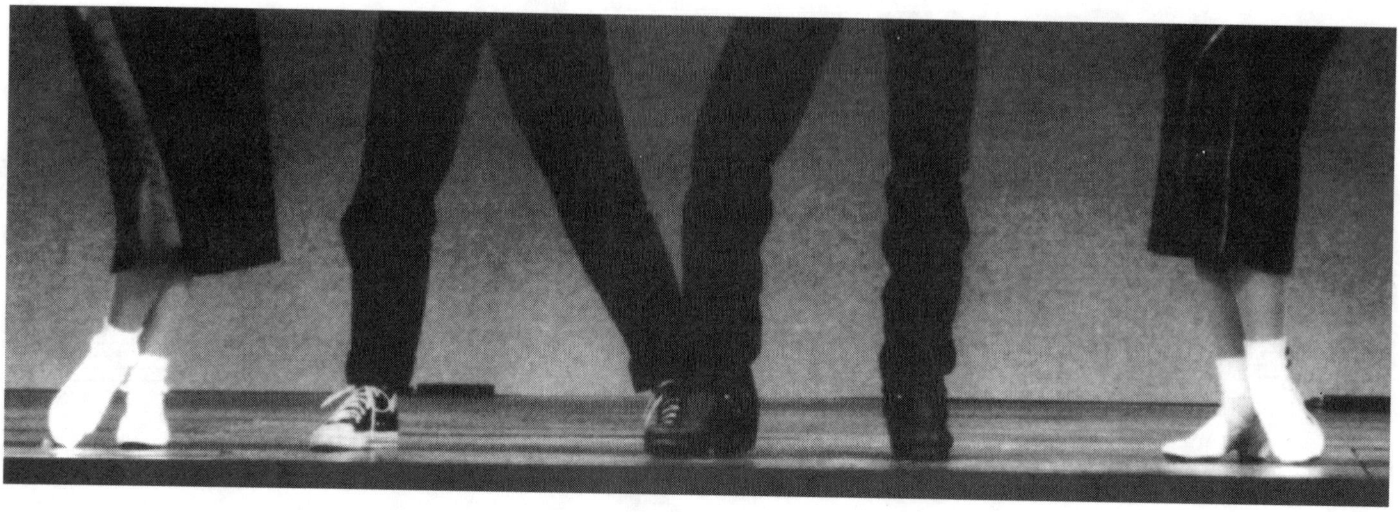

Mooning

Lyric and Music by WARREN CASEY
and JIM JACOBS

Moderately slow

Em C D7 C
Oh, I'm so full of
All o-ver who?
D7 Bm Em
love, as an-y fool can see, 'cause
A F♯7 Bm
An-gels up a-bove have hu-u-ung a
C D7 G Em
moon on me. Why must I go on

C D7 G
Moon - - - ing so all a - lone?
Em C D7 G
There would be no
(So all a - lone)
Em C D7
more Moon - - - ing if you would
G Em C D7
call me. Oh,
(Up on the phone)

C D7 Bm E7
ly-ing by my-self in bed I cry and give my-self the red eye,
C D7 G D7 Rubato
Moon- - -ing o-ver you. I'll stand be-
(Rubato)
G Em C D7
hind you, Moon- - -ing for-ev-er-
G Em C D7
more. Some-day you'll
(For-ev-er - more)

G Em C D7
find me Moon - - - ing at your front
G Em C D7
door. Oh,
(At my front door)
C D7 Bm E7
ev-'ry day at school I watch ya, Al-ways will un-til I got-cha
C D7 G C Cm G Gmaj7
Moon - - - ing too. There's a moon out to-night.
rit.

Look At Me, I'm Sandra Dee

Lyric and Music by WARREN CASEY
and JIM JACOBS

2
G7 C C7 Fm7 B♭7
Dor - is Day. I don't drink or swear, I don't
E♭ Cm7 Dm7 G7 C
rat my hair, I get ill from one cig - ar - ette,
C7 Fm7 B♭7 C A7
Keep your filth - y paws off my silk - y drawers, would you
D G G7
pull that stuff with An - nette?

C C7 F D
As for you, Troy Don - a - hue, I know
No, no, no, Sal Min - e - o, I would
G G7 C C7
what you wan - na do, You got your crust, I'm no
nev - er stoop so low, Please keep your cool, now you're
F 1 D7 C G7 C
ob - ject of lust, I'm just plain San - dra Dee.
start - ing to
2 D7 C G7 C
drool, fon - gool, I'm San - dra Dee.

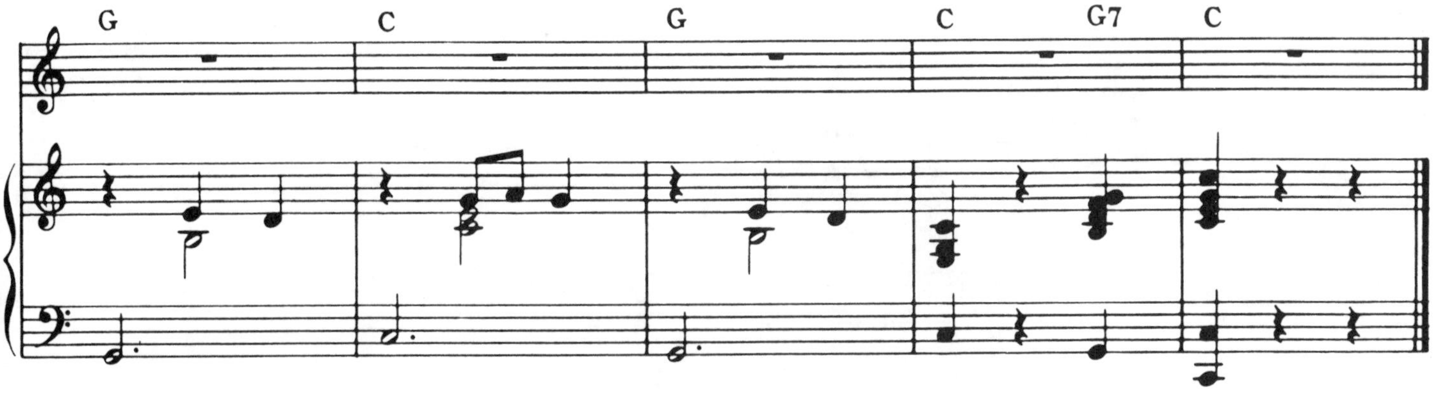

REPRISE: EXTRA LYRIC

Look at me, there has to be
Something more than what they see
Wholesome and pure, also scared and unsure
A poor man's Sandra Dee.
When they criticize and make fun of me,
Can't they see the tears in my smile?
Don't they realize there's just one of me,
And it has to last me awhile.

Sandy, you must start anew,
Don't you know what you must do?
Hold your head up high, take a deep breath and cry
Goodbye
To Sandra Dee.

We Go Together

Lyric and Music by WARREN CASEY
and JIM JACOBS

Moderate Rock in 2

C
Am
F
We Go To - geth - er, like ra - ma la - ma la - ma ka
We're one of a kind like dip da dip da dip
G
C
Am
ding - a da ding - dong, Re - mem - bered for - ev - er as
doo wop - a doo - bee doo, our names are signed
F
G
shoo - bop - sha - wad - da wad - da yip - pi - ty boom de - boom
boog - e - dy boog - e - dy boog - e - dy boog - e - dy shoo - by doo wop she bop

C Am F G7
chang chang ah chang-it-ty chang-shoo bop, that's the way it should
chang chang ah chang-it-ty chang-shoo bop, we'll al-ways bee - ee like
1
C Am F G
be, wha oooh, yeah!
2
C F C C7 F
one. Wa - wa - wa - waaah. When we go
C
out at night, and stars are shin - ing bright up in the

C7
F
skies a - bove.
Or at the
D
high school dance, where you can find ro-mance, may - be it
Opt. G
(Scat singing ad lib.)
C
Am
might be love.
C
Am
F
G7
We're for each oth - er like-a wop ba-ba lu-mop and wop bam boom.

C Am F
Just like my broth - er is sha - na - na na - na - na,
G7 C Am
yip - pi - ty dip - de doom chang chang ah chang - it - ty chang - shoo bop,
F G7 C Am F G7
We'll al-ways be to - geth - er, to - geth - er.
Repeat (scat singing and fade)
C Am F G

It's Raining On Prom Night

Lyric and Music by WARREN CASEY
and JIM JACOBS

A7 D Bm G
mess, It's run-ning all o-ver my taf - fe-ta
A7 D Bm G
dress, It's wilt-ing the quilt-ing in my Maid-en-
A7 D Bm G
form and mas-ca-ra flows right down my nose, be - cause of the
3
A7 D G F♯m7
storm. I don't e - ven have my cor - sage, Oh,

D7 G B7/F♯
gee, it fell down_ a sew - er___ with my
Em A7 D Bm
sis - ter's_ I. D. It's Rain-ing___ On Prom Night,_ Oh,
G A7 D Bm
what can I do.___ It's rain-ing___ rain from the skies, it's
G A7 D B♭7
rain-ing___ tears from my eyes_ o - ver you._ It's

E♭ Cm A♭
Rain-ing On Prom Night, Oh, What can I
B♭7 E♭ Cm
do? It's rain-ing rain from the skies, it's
A♭ B♭7 E♭ Cm
rain-ing tears from my eyes o-ver you. Rain-ing,
A♭ B♭7 E♭
rain-ing, rain-ing on Prom night, rain-ing.

Born To Hand Jive

Lyric and Music by WARREN CASEY
and JIM JACOBS

G A G A G A G A G A G A
stom-ach bounc-ing all a - round._ 'Cause a
D E D E D E C D C D C D
be - bop stork was 'bout to ar-rive,___ ma-ma gave birth to the hand jive._
G A G A G A G A G A G A
I could
G A G A G A G A G A G A
bare - ly walk when I milked a cow,_ And when

G A G A G A G A G A G A
I was three, I pushed a plow. While
C D C D C D C D C D C D
chop-ping wood I'd move my legs, and
G A G A G A G A G A G A
start-ed danc-in' while I gath-ered eggs, The
D E D E D E C D C D C D
town folk clapped, I was on-ly five, he'll out dance 'em all, he's a born hand jive.

Repeat and improvise freely (over 10 bars blues)
G A G A G A G A G A G A
Doo-dle-ee doo-dle-ee doo doo Doo-dle-ee doo-dle-ee doo doo
G A G A G A G A G A G A
Doo-dle-ee doo-dle-ee doo doo Doo-dle-ee doo-dle-ee doo doo
A G A G A G A G A
Born to hand jive, ba-by. Born to hand jive, ba-by.
Repeat and improvise freely (over 10 bars blues)
G A G A G A G A G A G A G A
oh, yeah, here_ we go. Doodle-ee doodle-ee doo doo Doodle-ee doodle-ee doo doo

EXTRA LYRIC:

So I grew up dancing on the stage
Doing the hand jive became the rage.
But a jealous stud, he pulled a gun
And said let's see how fast you can run.
Yeah!
Natural rhythm kept me alive,
Out dodgin' bullets with the old hand jive.
Now can you hand jive, baby,
Oh, can you hand jive, baby.

Beauty School Dropout

Lyric and Music by WARREN CASEY
and JIM JACOBS

2
E7
A
F♯m
D
Beau-ty School Drop-out, no grad-u - a - tion day for
Drop-out, hang-in' a-round the cor-ner
ya.
mp
you, Beau-ty School Drop-out, missed your mid-terms and flunked sham-
store, Beau-ty School Drop-out, it's a-bout time you knew the
poo, Well, at least you could have tak - en time to wash and clean your
score, Well, they could-n't teach you an - y-thing, you think you're such a
clothes up, aft-er spend-ing all that dough to have the doc - tor fix your
look-er, but no cus-tom-er would go to you, un-less she was a

to Coda
E7 A F♯m D
nose up, Ba-by, get mov-in', why keep your fee - ble hopes a -
hook-er, Ba-by, don't
E7 A F♯m D
live, What are ya prov-in'? You got the dream, but not the
E7 A A+ D
drive. If you go for your di - plo-ma, you could join a sten - o -
Dm A F♯m D E7 A E7
D.𝄋 al Coda
pool, Turn in your teas-ing comb and go back to high school. Beau-ty School

A
F♯m
D
sweat it, ___ you're not cut out to hold a
CODA
E7
A
F♯m
job, ___ Bet - ter for - get it, ___ who wants their
D
E7
A
hair done by a slob? ___ Now, your bangs are curled, your
A+
D
Dm
Rubato
lash - es twirled, but still the world is cruel. Wipe off that

A F♯m D E7 A
an - gel face and go back to high__ school.____
D Dm E7 A
Ya ooh.____

Alone At The Drive-In Movie

Lyric and Music by WARREN CASEY
and JIM JACOBS

G
C
were - wolves without you.
F
G (Tacet) rubato
C
a tempo
Owoooo, owoooo
(Wolf howl)
Gee, it's no fun
rubato
a tempo
F
G
C
drink - ing beer in the back - seat,
F
G
C
All a - lone just ain't too neat,

F G C F
at the pas - sion pit want-ing you.
C C7 F G
Owoooo, owoooo And when the in - ter-mis - sion elf moves the
C F G
clock's hands, When he's eat-ing ev-'ry-thing sold at the
C F G
stand, When there's one min-ute to go 'til the

C
Am
F
lights go down low, I'll be hold-ing the speak - er knobs, miss-ing you
G
rubato
C
a tempo
so. I can't be - lieve it,
rubato
a tempo
F
G
C
Un - steamed win-dows I can see through,
F
G
C
Might as well be in an ig - loo,

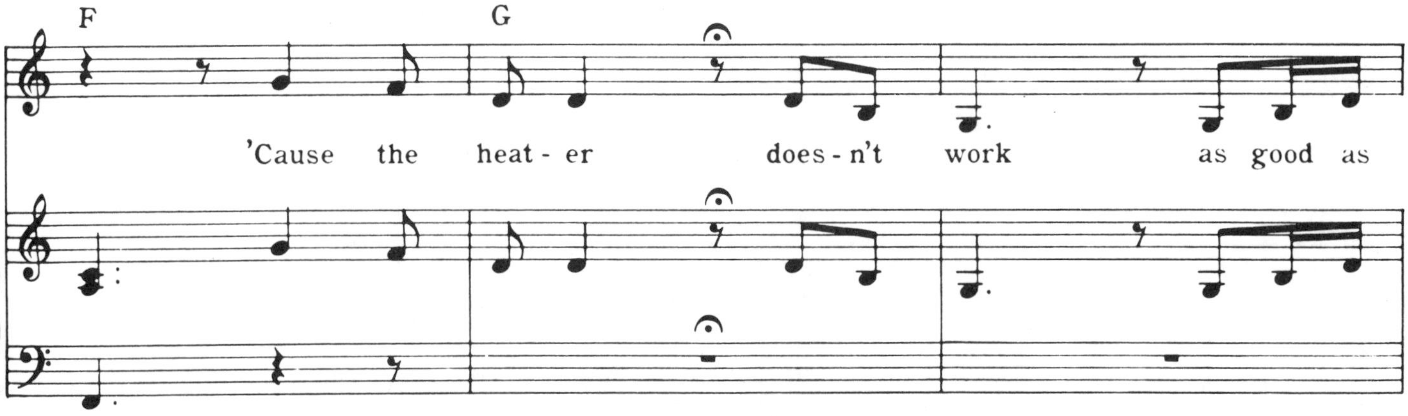
F
G
'Cause the heat - er does - n't work as good as

C
F
C
Cmaj9
you.
(Ba - by come back.)

1955
1957
R

Rock 'N' Roll Party Queen

Lyric and Music by WARREN CASEY
and JIM JACOBS

F
B♭
C
F
2. Fri-day night and she's got a date,
Go - in' plac-es, just-a
3. She's the girl that all the kids know,
Talk a-bout her where
B♭
C
F
B♭
C
stay-in' out late,
Drop-pin' dimes in the record ma-chine, Ah, ho, ho,
ev-er she goes
I could write a fan mag-a-zine a-bout my
F
B♭
F
F7
B♭
Rock 'N' Roll Pa-ar-ty Queen
Pa, pa, pa, pa, pa,
Rock 'N' Roll Pa-ar-ty Queen
Bomp ba-bomp ba-bomp
Dm
Oh, no, can I have the car to night?
You should see her shake to the la - test dance,

Gm
Bay - bee, bay bee, can I be the one to
Bay - bee, bay bee, no, don't call it pup-py love, Don't
C
love you with all a my mi - hite?
cha wan-na tru - hu ro - man - hance? Oh,
C7
Ay, yi, yi, yi.
F
Rock-in' and a-roll-in' lit-tle
B♭ C
par - ty queen, we
F
gon-na do the stroll, you' my
B♭ C
par - ty queen. Ya
F
know I love you so, hey,
B♭ C
par - ty queen, you're my

B♭
C
F
Rock-in' and a - roll-in' par-ty queen.

There Are Worse Things I Could Do

Lyric and Music by WARREN CASEY
and JIM JACOBS

1.
2.
C C7 C Cm Ab
do. I could do. I could stay home ev-'ry night,
Bb7 Ebmaj7 Ab
Wait a-round for Mis-ter Right, Take cold
All. (Sit and
Fm G7
show-ers ev-'ry day And throw my life a-way For a
watch my hair turn gray)
Cm Cm/Bb C7 Am7 C Dm
dream that won't come true. I could hurt some-one like me

Dm/C Bb Em7-5 A9
Out of spite or jeal-ous-y. I don't
Dmaj7 D6 Gm A7
steal and I don't lie but I can feel and I can cry, A fact I'll bet you nev-er
Dm9 Dm/C Bb Gm6
knew. But to cry in front of you,
C7 C7sus4 C7 F Bb6 Bbm6 F
That's the worst thing I could do.

All Choked Up

Lyric and Music by WARREN CASEY
and JIM JACOBS

B♭
knees are weak, and my back - bone quakes. My hands are
C
cold - er than ice my throat is locked in a vice, Come on and
3
3
F
F7
B♭
change my pain to par - a - dise. Well there's a fev - er heat run - nin'
B♭7
thru my skin don't you hear me knock - in', oh, won't you let me in. You

E♭ F E♭ F E♭ F
know I'm your fool, so don't you be cruel, uh huh, I'm All Choked Up.
B♭ B♭7 E♭
Chorus: (Now lis-ten here.) So you're spin-nin' round in a di-iz-zy spell, it's a
Girl: down and out, you're a-ga-ainst the wall and you're
E♭7 A♭ B♭
si-it-u-a-tion I know pret-ty well. Well I've been there too, so,
say-in' I'm the one that did it all. Well, I'm sure you're sin-cere, it
A♭ B♭ A♭ B♭ 1 E♭
I feel for you, uh huh, I'm All Choked Up. (And furth-er more.) So you're
gets me right here, uh huh, I'm All Choked Up.

2
E♭ E♭7 A♭ E♭
— Oh, ba - by, take it slow— and don't com - plain, my
A♭ E♭ F
poor heart just can't stand the strain. I can cure your dis - ease. Come on and
B♭ B♭7
say pret - ty please, take you're med - i - cine down— on — your knees.
E♭ D♭ C♭ B♭ E♭ D♭
Boy: Got a fev - er, a hun-dred four— fahr - en - heit, need your lov - in'

C♭ B♭ E♭ D♭ C♭ B♭
can I come o-ver to-night? Feel-in' low-down, my e-qui-li-bri-um's shot
E♭ D♭ C♭ B♭ E♭
gim-me gim - me that tran-quil-i-zer you got.
B7 E
Oh, ba-by take my ring, 'cause you're my match. Girl: Well,
B C♯
I still think there's strings at-tached. You're writ-ing my e-pi-taph. Well, that's just
Boy:
Girl:

F♯
F♯7
tough and a half _ You're gon - na make me die, _ Don't make me laugh. Well, I
Boy:
Girl:
Both:
B
might for - give _ what you put me thru, _ 'cause I do be - lieve you real - ly
B7
E
F♯
E
F♯
love me too. _ I look in your eyes, _ the suf - fer - ing dies, _ uh
E
F♯
B
E
F♯
huh, I'm All Choked Up. ___ Hey, hey, hey, hey, I'm All Choked Up. _

B
E
F♯
B
Hey, hey, hey, hey, I'm All Choked Up.